For information contact
Rosalind Warren, Laugh Lines Press,
P.O. Box 259, Bala Cynwyd, PA 19004
215-668-4252

Author's photograph by
Mario De Meideros

Printed in U.S.A.

Library of Congress
Catalog Card Number
93-080906

Stand Back, I Think I'm Gonna Laugh. . .
p.   cm

ISBN
0-9632526-3-1

1. Humor
2. Women's Studies—humor

I. Rina Piccolo, 1966–

Stand Back,
I Think I'm Gonna
Laugh . . .

To my Grandfather
who always made me laugh
and
a special thank you to Roz
who made this book happen

13

BRIDGE OVER TROUBLED WATERS

IN ONE BIZARRE FLEETING INSTANT HE FELT A TOE BOLT IN AND OUT OF HIS MOUTH.

"BOY, HAVE I GOT AN INCREDIBLY OVER-POWERING URGE TO SCREW ANYTHING THAT MOVES...!" BLURTED HANK.

JACK OFTEN LIT-UP AFTER MEALS.

47

50

SPERM WARFARE

71

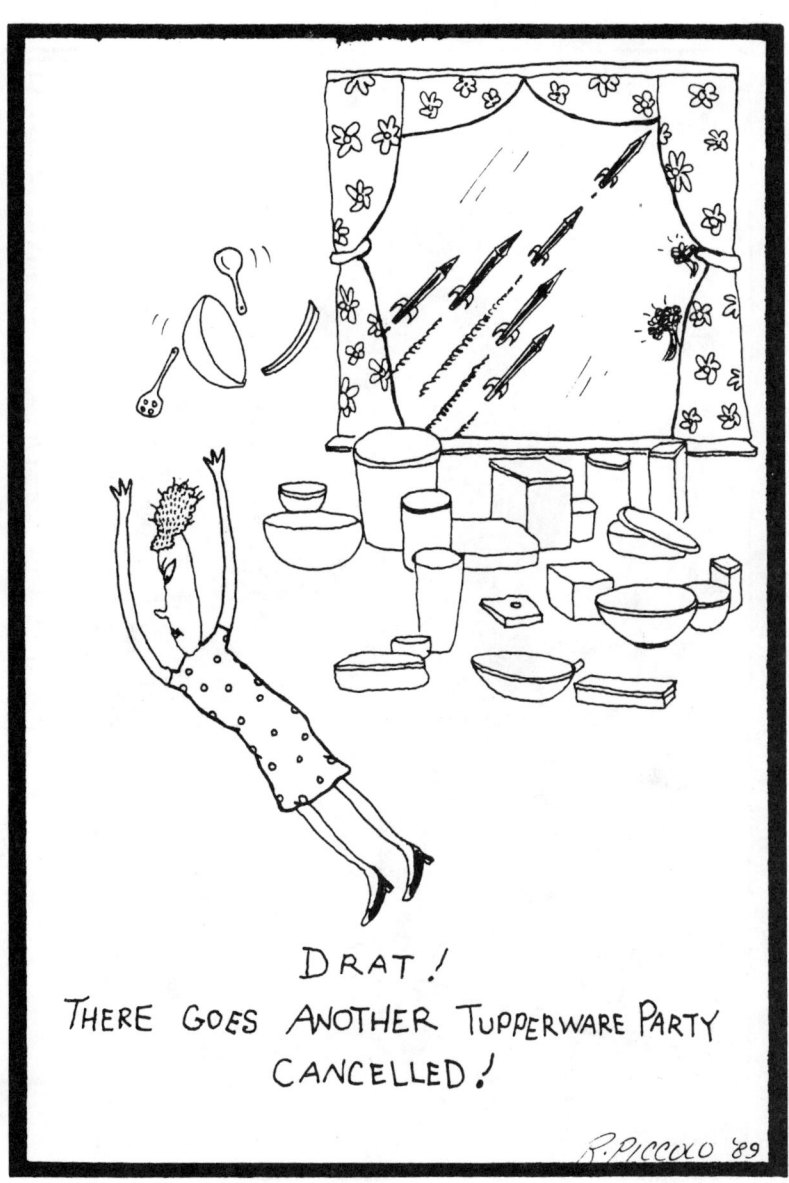

DRAT!
THERE GOES ANOTHER TUPPERWARE PARTY
CANCELLED!

R.PICCOLO '89

.... WE NOW HAVE CONCLUSIVE SCIENTIFIC EVIDENCE THAT THE UNIVERSE DID NOT BEGIN WITH A BIG BANG ..... IT ACTUALLY WENT LIKE THIS... HIT IT BOYS!
R. PICCOLO

AT 40 SECOND INTERVALS, BECKY CHECKS FOR THE LITTLE STRING